EXECUTING YOUR LEADERSHIP ASSIGNMENT

ANDRE THOMAS

GREATNESS PUBLISHING

www.12leadersmovement.com

Published by Greatness Publishing, Ontario, Canada

Cover design by Farouk Roberts

Library and Archives Canada

ISBN 978-1-927579-24-4

All Scripture quotations are from the New King James Version of the Bible, except otherwise stated.

www.greatnesspublishing.com

ACKNOWLEDGEMENTS

I wish to thank the Lord Jesus Christ for entrusting me with the revelation of the 12 spheres of leadership.

Thanks also to my wife and ministry partner who typed this manuscript.

CONTENTS

CHAPTER ONE

The Season of Manifestation

And thou, child, shalt be called the prophet of the Highest: for thou shalt go before the face of the Lord to prepare his ways; To give knowledge of salvation unto his people by the remission of their sins, Through the tender mercy of our God; whereby the dayspring from on high hath visited us, To give light to them that sit in darkness and in the shadow of death, to guide our feet into the way of peace. And the child grew, and waxed strong in spirit, and was in the deserts till the day of his shewing unto Israel. Luke 1:76-80.

When the angel of the Lord came to Zacharias and revealed the leadership assignment of his son John, the destiny of John did not manifest instantly. Luke 1:18 reveals that there was a stage of preparation in which he grew and waxed strong in spirit and was in the desert/wilderness until the day the execution of his mission was to begin.

The day the execution of your assignment should begin is not only defined by God but is affected by your obedience and your yielding to the process of God. There are things that God has ordained for you that will be delayed by your reluctance to yield to the divine process. Many people never step into the execution phase of their assignment and in this chapter we will examine some of the reasons why.

The first one is **perpetual wilderness relationships**.
There are people who are born in the wilderness and will die in the wilderness. There are families in which no one has ever graduated from the school of the wilderness. These people have a mentality and a language that keeps them in the wilderness perpetually. The scripture tells us that *he that walketh with wise men shall become wise but a companion of fools shall be destroyed.* Proverbs 13:20.

Wise people are creative people and they take vision from concept to reality. Fools are dreamers who never wake up from their dreams to do what is required to cause their dreams and visions to come to pass. When your relationships and counsel is from men and women who have never possessed nor inherited the promises of God for their lives they are doomed. Association matters and you will become like those with whom you associate, whether it be friends or family. You will either rise to their level or fall to their level.

Many destinies are delayed because many do not know the atmosphere and mindset of a heavenly achiever. They only know the mindset and atmosphere of a survivor who works to exist and never fulfills their true potential. If you are born into such a family, if you are surrounded with friends like that, you must build new relationships and obey what the scripture says that is to follow those who through faith and patience inherited the promises. Hebrews 5:12.

Jesus built a team of 12 relationships that supported His destiny. Write down a list of relationships you have that you understand and will partner with you in the spirit to see your destiny come to pass. If you do not have any, pray until you have at least twelve.

1. _____
2. _____
3. _____
4. _____
5. _____
6. _____
7. _____
8. _____
9. _____
10. _____
11. _____
12. _____

A Lack of Vision

Vision is a clear mental portrait of a preferred future. Divine vision is a clear mental portrait of God's preferred future for a person. When a person does not discern, embrace and pursue the vision that God has for them, they always stay in the wilderness. It was God's vision that the children of Israel possessed Canaan

Land. However, the children of Israel did not embrace it and therefore stayed in the wilderness.

One a scale from 1 to 10 how clear is your vision of God's leadership assignment for your life?

Low	1	2	3	4	5	6	7	8	9	10	High

CHAPTER TWO

Focusing on the Assignment

But none of these things move me, neither do I count my life dear to myself, so that I might finish my course with joy, and the ministry which I received from the Lord Jesus Christ, to testify fully the gospel of the grace of God. Acts 20:24.

Focus is concentrating on the priorities that are required to acquire what you desire. Focus is made up of two major components:

1. Concentration
2. Priorities

Concentration is the ability to harness your strengths and utilize them for a single purpose.

Knowing your priorities is the other side of focus. It requires a comprehensive understanding of your assignment. Paul was a man of unusual focus and in the above scripture he makes the following statements:

1. None of these things move me.

What Paul is saying is the he is only moved into action by God, God's word and his assignment. He is not moved by what he feels or hears or sees, he is only moved by the word of God to him and his divinely given priorities.

List the priorities that God has given you in order to fulfill your assignment.

_____
_____
_____
_____
_____
_____

2. I do not count my life dear to myself.

An athlete who considers the feelings of his body as precious to him will never become a championship athlete. This is because your body usually does not feel to do what is right. Paul is using the language of an athlete by saying that winning the race of his destiny and crossing the finish line is his focus and not the way his body feels as it undergoes the stress of running the race of destiny.

List the stresses you must ignore to successfully run the race that is set before you.

_____

_____

_____

_____

_____

_____

3. That I might finish my course with joy and the ministry which I received from the Lord.

This is the language of a marathon runner whose body is feeling the effect of the marathon but is determined to endure the race and finish the course as a winner. The execution of your leadership assignment is a journey and having an attitude of joy would release the strength of God into your life to successfully execute all that God has for your life.

What are the joy boosters in your life that you need to embrace?

_____

_____

_____

_____

_____

_____

CHAPTER THREE

Execution Relationships

And in Antioch some among the existing church were prophets and teachers. (such as Barnabas, and Simeon who was called Niger, and Lucius of Cyrene, and Manaen, the foster-brother of Herod the tetrarch) and Saul. As they ministered to the Lord and fasted, the Holy Spirit said, So, then, separate Barnabas and Saul to Me for the work to which I have called them. Acts 13:1-2.

The above scripture reveals two major insights on the execution of leadership assignments.

1. When the Holy Spirit said to separate Paul and Barnabas for the work where unto I have called them, they had been in the ministry for over thirteen years. They were obviously in the preparation stage and were now about to step into the execution phase of their ministry.

Kenneth E. Hagin in his book *I Believe in Visions* gives an account of an encounter he had with the Lord of which he explained that many ministers live and die and never step into the first phase of what God has for them. After approximately thirteen years Paul and Barnabas stepped into their destiny work that God had reserved for them.

2.   Destiny is relationship and when the Holy Ghost spoke, He said separate Paul and Barnabas for the work that I have called them, therefore in implying that God calls but man separates and creates a space for you to fulfill your calling once you recognize it. The elders in the church at Antioch created a destiny platform of prayer, emotional support, financial and logistical support for Paul and Barnabas to fulfill their leadership assignment.

It is interesting to note that Paul's destiny relationship base was not Jerusalem. In fact in Jerusalem all he did was get himself arrested. However in Antioch his destiny was celebrated, embraced and supported. In Jerusalem his destiny was opposed. We also see that God sent out Paul in a team with Barnabas. He said separate Paul and Barnabas.

There are men and women that you must work with to execute your leadership assignment. Your season of preparation will help develop Christ in you so that you can develop life-giving relationships with your destiny partners.

List the names of your partners in the fulfillment of your destiny.

_____

_____

_____

_____

_____

_____

CHAPTER FOUR

Phases of Execution

But you shall receive power, the Holy Spirit coming upon you. And you shall be witnesses to Me both in Jerusalem and in all Judea, and in Samaria, and to the end of the earth. Acts 1:8.

The God that you serve is a God who accomplishes His vision in stages. As you partner with Him, your leadership assignment will be accomplished in phases as well. There are four factors that would impact your ability to successfully navigate the challenges of life and execute your leadership assignment in phases.

1. Partnership

The work of God is accomplished on the earth through a partnership relationship that God establishes with man through a covenant. We see that partnership at work at the creation of the first man. At the creation of the first man and the execution of his leadership assignment, the first thing we see is that God plants a garden in the earth call the Garden of Eden and He does not deploy angels to cultivate it but He asked His partner Adam to cultivate and guard the garden.

We also see God comes to His partner Adam, brings the animals to Adam and asks him to name them and whatever name Adam would give them, that is the name that would be accepted by God. A partnership suggests that two or more people are working together each making a unique contribution for the fulfillment of the vision of the relationship and the neutral benefit of each person.

A partnership does not mean that one person does everything. In your partnership with God, God is the Senior Partner and you are the junior partner and some things God will do and there are some things you must do in order for the agreed vision for the relationship happen. A partnership is not possible if:

a. There is no agreed vision.

It is impossible to be in partnership with God if you and God disagree over what the vision of your relationship must be. God as the Senior Partner in the relationship sets the vision and you agree to it. He also gives you the option of adding certain of your preferences to the vision like He did with Adam in the naming of the animals.

The story of Jonah is the story of a man who disagreed with God's vision of the partnership between Him and Jonah. Many make the mistake of Jonah and live their lives agreeing or running from God over the vision of their relationship. What is very clear from the scriptures is that if you wholeheartedly pursue God's vision for the partnership relationship with Him, He will give you the option and ask you in certain areas of your life "what do you want?" like he did with Solomon.

This level of favor with God is not available to the disobedient and the rebellious.

On a scale of 1 to 10 assess your level of understanding of the Holy Spirit's vision of the partnership between you and Him.

Low	1	2	3	4	5	6	7	8	9	10	High

On a scale of 1 to 10 assess your level of agreement and wholehearted pursuit of the Holy Spirit's vision of His partnership with you.

Low	1	2	3	4	5	6	7	8	9	10	High

b. There are no agreed values.

The Holy Spirit has a set of values that are called the fruit of the spirit and to have a great relationship with Him you have got to walk in those values as well.

On a scale of 1 to 10 assess the measure of each fruit of the spirit in your life:

Values that benefit you:

i.   Love – Giving of you for the benefit of others.

Low	1	2	3	4	5	6	7	8	9	10	High

ii.   Joy – An excitement about living that comes from within and is not based on external circumstances.

Low	1	2	3	4	5	6	7	8	9	10	High

iii.   Peace – A state of emotional and mental harmony and the absence of conflict within.

Low	1	2	3	4	5	6	7	8	9	10	High

Values that benefit others:

iv.   Longsuffering – The ability to patiently endure wrongs and difficulties with a good attitude.

Low	1	2	3	4	5	6	7	8	9	10	High

v.   Goodness – The practice of adding value to everyone you come in contact with.

Low	1	2	3	4	5	6	7	8	9	10	High

vi.   Kindness – The practice of treating people in a tender, sensitive and humane way.

Low	1	2	3	4	5	6	7	8	9	10	High

Values that benefit God:

vii.   Meekness – The practice of adjusting your life to the truth and divine direction once it is revealed.

Low	1	2	3	4	5	6	7	8	9	10	High

viii.   Self-Control – The practice of subduing your feelings, words, thoughts and actions to behave in a Christ-like manner.

Low	1	2	3	4	5	6	7	8	9	10	High

ix.   Faithfulness – Unwavering devotion and loyalty to Gods Word, and divine principles, assignments and relationships

Low	1	2	3	4	5	6	7	8	9	10	High

c. There is no win-win relationship.

True partnerships are by nature neutrally beneficial and God is committed to ensuring that you win out of the partnership with him. He states in His Word that He is a rewarder of them that diligently seek Him. Hebrews 11:6. But without faith *it is* impossible to please *Him*, for he who comes to God must believe that He is and *that* He is a rewarder of those who diligently seek Him.

However, God is not interested in a lose-win partnership where you are the winner and He is the loser. He wants to benefit from the relationship and see an aspect of His Will done in your life through your passionate obedience.

One a scale of 1 to 10 accesses how much God has benefited from His partnership with you.

Low	1	2	3	4	5	6	7	8	9	10	High

1. Addiction to divine direction

The anointing of God on your life is no substitute for divine direction. You may be very anointed today but if you make the wrong moves, you can become ex-anointed tomorrow. Those who follow the Lord, always grow from glory to glory. Proverbs 4:18. *But the path of the just is as the shining light, that shineth more and more unto the perfect day.*

2. Continuous improvement and personal growth

Success is a perishable asset and the success you have today can be gone tomorrow if you do not keep improving.

- There was a day when Lucifer was very successful as he executed the will of God but he fell into failure.
- There was a day when Adam was very successful but he fell into failure.
- There was a day when Eve was very successful but she fell into failure.
- There was a day when Saul was very successful but he fell into failure.
- There was a day when Uzziah was very successful but he fell into failure.
- There was a day when Samson was very successful but he fell into failure.
- There was a day that Judas was successful but he fell into failure.

Stop, reflect and list the things that need to be operational in your life to prevent you from falling into failure.

_____

_____

_____

_____

_____

_____

3. Spiritual understanding

The spiritual understanding is seen in the spirit what is required to acquire what you desire. Understanding is key because what you do not understand you cannot maximize. You must understand your leadership assignment and the gifts you have been given to fulfill it and the partners that you have been given to execute it.

Let's look deeper at the key things you must understand to maximize your assignment. I will use my life and the life of Esther to explain this.

1. To whom are you assigned?
   Esther – she was assigned to the nation of Israel.
   Me – I am assigned to people and nations in bondage.
   You:_____

   _____

   _____

   _____

   _____

   _____

2. Who has assigned you?
   Esther – God assigned her.
   Me – God assigned me.
   You:_____

   _____

   _____

   _____

   _____

   _____

3. What is the task of your assignment?
   Esther – to deliver and preserve the destiny of Israel.
   Me – to take a people from bondage to greatness.
   You:_____

   _____

   _____

   _____

   _____

   _____

4. What are the gifts that God has given you to execute your assignment?
   Esther – the gifts of a political leadership, political diplomacy and outstanding physical beauty.
   Me – miracle ministry, wisdom ministry, leadership development ministry and strategy consultant.
   You:_____

   _____

   _____

   _____

   _____

   _____

5. What is the relational platform for your assignment?
   Esther – Queen of Persia and Media.

Me – Founder of Fresh Anointing and Wisdom Network, Greatness Publishing and Andre Thomas Strategy Consulting.

You:_____

_____

_____

_____

_____

_____

6. Who are the partners in your assignment?

Esther – her husband the king, Mordecai and her assigned palace staff.

Me – my wife, my daughters, my staff team, 12 leaders movement partners, city wide revival partners and ministry, prayer, government leaders, board of directors/business partners and financial partners.

You:_____

_____

_____

_____

_____

_____

CHAPTER FIVE

Execution Mistakes

Now unto him that is able to keep you from falling, and to present you faultless before the presence of his glory with exceeding joy, To the only wise God our Saviour, be glory and majesty, dominion and power, both now and ever. Amen. Jude 1:24-25.

Anyone can fall from their place of glory in the kingdom of God to a lower level or into hell itself. There are three major reason why people fall from there place of execution to a lower level of execution, back into the wilderness phase, sometimes into hell itself or get disqualified from the race of destiny.

There are divine mandate mistakes, leadership mistakes and holiness mistakes.

Divine Mandate Mistakes

For Herod had laid hold on John, and had bound him, and had put him in prison because of Herodias his brother Philip's wife. For John said to him, it is not lawful for you to have her. And when he desired to put him to death, he feared the multitude, because they counted him as a prophet. But when Herod's birthday was kept, the daughter of Herodias danced before them and pleased Herod. So he promised with an oath to give her whatever she would ask. And she, being instructed before by her mother, said, give me John the Baptist's head here on a platter. And the king was sorry. But for the oath's sake, and those reclining with him, he commanded it to be given. And he sent and beheaded John in the prison. And his head was brought on a platter and given to the girl. And she brought it to her mother. Matthew 14:3-11.

A divine mandate is an assignment that is given by the God of the Universe to a person, family, organization or nation to execute and by its very nature has the full backing of the power influence and protection of the throne of God and all its resources.

John the prophet whom Jesus referred to as the greatest prophet in the Old Testament, had a divine mandate to be a prophetic voice crying in the wilderness, making ready a path for the coming of the Lord Jesus Christ.

While he executed this heavenly assignment no weapon formed against him could prosper, for he was standing in the secret place of the Most High. This secret place is the divine role that God had assigned him to and he did it with distinction.

As he stood in his place, the conditional promises of Psalm 91 were his portion and no evil befell him. However, something happened when Jesus began His ministry and John lost focus during this process of transition and he allowed his passion to correct a wrong that he saw in the life of Herod the king to get the better of him.

John was not a prophet in the order of Nathan who could walk into a king's palace and speak truth to political power that was inconvenient and walk away without his head being cut off. John was a prophet who was called to be a forerunner. He was not a prophet in the order of Daniel who could speak to the greatest political leader of his day and tell him that God was going to judge him and that he would crawl like an animal and eat grass and walk away without his [Daniel's] head being cut off.

When John decided to step out of the jurisdiction of his divine mandate and declare publicly that it was unlawful for Herod to marry the woman that he did, the angels of God did not have a mandate to protect him from the backlash that resulted. He had stepped out of his sphere of authority and was on his own. John was arrested and later was cruelly executed.

Think about it; John came in the spirit and power of Elijah. Can you imagine a king executing Elijah, a man who had the authority to call down fire from heaven and burn up soldiers sent to arrest him? I am sure you cannot. This was John's authority if he had stayed within his jurisdiction.

To help you understand this, let's use an example from the army as you and I are in the army of the Lord. If you are the leader of an elite special operations team and you are sent into a country called Lobutoo to destroy the power stations in readiness for a full blooded air assault, you will be given air support in the form of:

1. Attack and rescue helicopters that you could call upon.
2. Unmanned predator drone that would provide surveillance and conduct attacks if necessary.
3. Air strike support in the form of bombers.

All these would be at your fingertips for the mission to Lobutoo and will be deployed within easy access to its airspace. However, if you on your own without the consultation and endorsement of your superiors decided to go on a different mission that was a hundred miles from Lobutoo and destroy bonkers in an island called Jaboya, and while you are on the island and called for air support you are on your own as there would be no deployment of the US army resources near that island.

If you make it out, it would entirely be due to your survival instincts and if you die it is not the fault of the US Army as you went outside of the jurisdiction of your assignment. This happens to many saints and they may not get their head chopped off like John, but they could get their finances, marriages, health, business, children and other aspects of their lives devastated by the forces of darkness because they have stepped outside of the divine cover of the Almighty God. David the king never made this mistake and was never defeated in battle because for every battle that he fought he received a divine mandate to do it.

Give an example of an incident in scripture where a person or people stepped outside of a divine mandate and got defeated.

_____

_____

_____

_____

_____

_____

What is the jurisdiction of your assignment? Example, my jurisdiction is to take people, families, organizations and nations from bondage to greatness. What is yours?

_____

_____

_____

_____

_____

Have you ever made a divine mandate mistake? If you have please state what it was and what was the painful price you paid.

_____

_____

_____

_____

_____

Leadership Mistakes

Leadership is using influence to work with and through people to accomplish a vision. Leadership mistakes occur in two ways:

1. When we disconnect from working with and through divine relationships because of our feelings and other issues.
2. When we chose to work with and through the wrong people.

Disconnecting From Divine Relationships

When you disconnect from divine relationships you always suffer. When you break up a team that God has put together for your benefit you will suffer great pain. None of us are immune from this folly and Paul one of the greatest men in the New Testament made the same mistake when he disconnected from a majestic and marvelous divine relationship with Barnabas over disagreement about Mark.

Also Paul and Barnabas continued in Antioch, teaching and preaching the gospel, the Word of the Lord, with many others also. And some days afterward, Paul said to Barnabas, Let us go again and visit our brothers in every city where we have announced the Word of the Lord, to see how they are holding to it. And Barnabas determined to take with them John, he being called Mark. But Paul thought it well not to take that one with them, he having withdrawn from them from Pamphylia, and did not go with them to the work. Then there was sharp feeling, so as to separate them from each other. And taking Mark, Barnabas sailed to Cyprus. But choosing Silas, Paul went out, being commended by the brothers to the grace of God, passing through Syria and Cilicia, making the churches strong. Acts 15:35-41.

God had handpicked, built and nurtured the team of Paul and Barnabas. Barnabas was the man that God used to bring Paul into a network of relationships that matched his destiny. Nobody in the church world at that time wanted to deal with Paul; however, Barnabas had great credibility and had almost as much influence as the apostles of the land who had walked with Jesus.

His level of influence, credibility, anointing and stature were only one notch less than the apostles. He was noted by the spirit of God as a man of distinction in financing the agenda of God right in the beginning days of the early church. He was an extremely anointed compassionate, merciful, Christ-like and very influential apostle of God.

Paul in the beginning days of his ministry only got to be accepted in certain places because of Barnabas's credibility and influence. It was Barnabas who invited Paul to become part of the move of God in Antioch. This was the church from which Paul's leadership assignment was released to his generation.

Mark on the other hand was a relative of Barnabas and when he made a mistake, Barnabas extended to him the same mercy that he had shown Paul. Mark later becomes one of the most influential Christian leaders in the history of the world and was chosen by the Holy Spirit to write the Gospel of Mark.

When Paul decided to disconnect from both of them and chose Silas who was not a man of the same caliber, influence, anointing and wealth, the caliber of the team fell and Paul went through excruciating hardships as a result of having a good but weaker person as his partner.

It is interesting to know that the Holy Spirit never chose Silas to work with Paul. The scripture recalls that he was recommended by the brethren and on their first mission together; they ended up in jail in Philippi and ended up being flogged only to be rescued by the intervention of the mercy of God.

Silas was a prophet and not an apostle like Barnabas and so the gift mix of the team that the Holy Ghost had put together was compromised. God wanted a team of two apostles and not a team of a prophet and an apostle. Only eternity will reveal the battles and agonies that Paul had to face because he lacked the stronger partnership with Barnabas. Somewhere in the scriptures Silas disappears and we hear no more from him.

Satan understands the power of divine relationships and will attack them to cause our assignments to be halted, delayed or become an exercise in pain and frustration. To maintain divine relationships you need to become a person who is meek, longsuffering and endeavors to keep the unity of the spirit and the bond of peace.

How do you access your level to keep the bond of peace with divine relationships during challenging times?

Low	1	2	3	4	5	6	7	8	9	10	High

Choosing to work with and through people that are against your destiny.

Life is a warfare and God's method to bless us is man and Satan's method to defeat us is also man. *One of the lessons I have learned is that both your friends and your enemies want to be close to you.* The story of David and Absalom is a story of a father who rightly loved his son and wrongly brought him to close to him and paid a high price for it.

- Absalom had sex with his father's concubines on the roof of the palace in the presence of Israel.
- Absalom launched a civil war and took over his father's throne.
- Absalom pursued his father to kill him.
- Absalom took over the government of Israel by cunning craftiness and force.
- Absalom intentionally created disloyalty against David.
- Absalom caused David to run for his life.

How did this happened you may ask. Well, David ignored all the signs of disloyalty to him and his family. When Absalom killed his brother Amnon because of the rape of his sister Tamar, he showed deep disloyalty to his father and to the family. He could have dealt with it differently and consulted with his father to punish Amnon for his crime and compensate his sister.

This tendency to act without consideration for his father and the family grew from a seed and became a giant oak tree that would later produce fruit that almost destroyed David's throne and life.

There are sinful habits that can be worked through with your partners in destiny, however the sin of disloyalty to you and the vision has the potential to cause more devastation than any other sin. There is a word for disloyal people in the constitution of most countries. It is called traitor for which many countries reserve the death penalty.

Absalom was a charismatic, talented, outstanding, disloyal leader and partner to his father David. The scriptures reveal to us that no relationship on earth is exempt from the spirit of a traitor. The first traitor was Cain. He killed his brother. Absalom was a son to David and his greatest traitor while Judas was a treacherous treasurer.

STET....*Tamar. And now do not let my lord the king take the thing to his heart, to the watch lifted up his eyes and looked. And, behold, many And Jonadab, the son of David's brother Shimeah answered and said, Let not my lord think that they have killed all the young men, the king's sons. For only Amnon is dead. For by the mouth of Absalom this has been determined from the day that he humbled his sister think that all the king's sons are dead, for only Amnon is dead. But Absalom fled. And the young man that kept people came by the way of the hillside behind him. And Absalom fled and went to Geshur, and was there three years. And King*

David longed to go forth to Absalom, for he was comforted about Amnon, since he was dead. 2Samuel 13:32-34, 38-39.

Traitors can arise in marriages, families, churches, organizations, friendships and governments. As stated earlier, no relationship is exempt. Traitors are traitors because they have agendas that do not reflect the agenda of the visions to which they claim loyalty.
You cannot complete your leadership assignment being suspicious of everyone around you. However what you have to do is to look for the opposite of disloyalty which is loyalty in the hearts and minds of people and work with those people. Disloyal people are normally disloyal to most people as they are only loyal to their selfish ambitions.

Give the gift of access to those who have proven their loyalty in spite of their relationship to you. Loyal people when they disagree with you will tell you because they value the relationship. However, disloyalty to the anointed does not go unpunished by God. Absalom died a terrible death.

Give examples of three people from the scriptures who were traitors to their destiny partners and the divine judgment they suffered as a result.

_____

_____

_____

_____

_____

_____

_____

_____

_____

_____

_____

_____

Look for loyalty and build divine relationships with loyal, competent and passionate people.

Holiness Mistakes

And Jehovah said to Samuel, Behold, I will do a thing in Israel at which both the ears of everyone who hears it shall tingle. In that day I will confirm to Eli all that which I have spoken as to his house, beginning and making an end. For I have told him that I will judge his house forever for the iniquity which he knows, because his sons made themselves vile and he did not restrain them. And therefore I have sworn to the house of Eli that the iniquity of Eli's house shall not be purged with sacrifice nor offering forever. 1 Samuel 3:11-14.

Eli sinned a great sin when he did not correct his sons and in the words of the Lord honored his sons above Him. Sin is a destiny destroyer and there are sins of the spirit and sins of the flesh. _Having therefore these promises, dearly beloved, let us cleanse ourselves from all filthiness of the flesh and spirit, perfecting holiness in the fear of God._ 2Corinthians 7:1.

Sins of the spirit occur when a person violates the natural order of God, rebels against divine commands and acts against the agenda of the kingdom of God. Examples:

- Moses hitting the rock twice with his rod as he disobeyed the command of God.
- Saul offering a sacrifice as a priest when he was called to be a king.
- David depending on his flesh and numbering the people.
- Eli honoring his sons above the commands of God.
- Judas betraying his destiny mentor Jesus Christ to the Pharisees.
- Ham not covering the nakedness of his father Noah but rather exposing it.
- Esau not honoring his birthright and selling it to Jacob.
- The idolatry of Israel.
- The rebellion of Jonah.
- The pride of Lucifer.
- Unforgiveness and bitterness.

Sins of the flesh occur when a person does not control their fleshy appetite and taste for evil and allows their feelings to drive them into breaking God's law. Examples:

- David sinning with Bathsheba.
- Samson sinning with Delilah.
- Noah getting drunk.
- Solomon and his many wives.

Are you more prone to the sins of the spirit or the sins of the flesh?

_____

_____

_____

_____

_____

_____

_____

_____

_____

_____

_____

CHAPTER SIX

Passion to Complete the Assignment

And this is life Jesus spoke these words and lifted up His eyes to Heaven and said, Father, the hour has come. Glorify Your Son so that Your Son also may glorify You, even as You have given Him authority over all flesh so that He should give eternal life to all You have given Him. And this is eternal, that they might know You, the only true God, and Jesus Christ whom You have sent. I have glorified You upon the earth. I have finished the work which You have given Me to do. John 17:1-4.

Jesus completed His assignment and so can you. Your dream when leaving the earth should be to come before the father and say, "Father I have completed the assignment that you have given me. Receive my spirit." This is the way to die. Keep running the race until you finish your assignment. Partner with the Holy Ghost and overcome the obstacles in your way.

Develop the mind of Christ in you and say with him that what sustains me is doing the will of God and waking up every morning to finish the assignment that He has given me. *Jesus said to them,*

My food is to do the will of Him who sent Me and to finish His work. John 4:34.

List seven attributes that must be in your life to enable you to complete the assignment God has entrusted in your hands.

_____

_____

_____

_____

_____

_____

_____

_____

_____

_____

_____

_____

OTHER BOOKS BY ANDRE THOMAS

Discovering Me
The Gift of Political Leadership
The Gift of Organizational Leadership
Unlock your Greatness
(A Young Leaders Handbook)
Uncommon Men and Distinguished Women
(A Rites of Passage Manual)
The 12 Spheres of Leadership

ABOUT THE 12 SPHERES OF LEADERSHIP MOVEMENT

PURPOSE

To raise up a global movement of the 12 types of leaders that shape the destinies of nations.

OUR MISSION

To influence and empower two million leaders globally to execute divine assignments in the 12 spheres of leadership.

OUR METHOD

Conferences

To form strategic partnerships with key national leaders to hold 12 Spheres of Leadership conferences, events and speaking engagements.

Media and Communication

1. We create media programs and a media platform to distribute 12 Spheres of Leadership Content to the World.
2. We communicate monthly to our partners through 'Leadership Fuel' a monthly audio teaching and news digest.

Books

We write, publish and distribute books that influence and empower leaders globally to execute divine assignments in the 12 spheres of leadership.

How can your church, town, city or nation be transformed by the 12 Spheres of Leadership Movement?

There are 3 different events that Bishop Andre Thomas may be booked for:

1.   LEADERSHIP WISDOM EXPLOSION

An event where:

- The biblical wisdom of the 12 Spheres of Leadership is imparted to equip the saints and to shape the destiny of their nation.

- Visionaries are refreshed by the Holy Spirit.

- This event can also be customized to focus on specific spheres of leadership

2.   ANOINTING REVIVAL

An event where:

- A fresh anointing is imparted to people individually and in mass to unlock their God given greatness.

- The delivering and healing power of God is also administered to set people free from all bondage.

3.   ANOINTING AND WISDOM CONFERENCE

This event features the best of Anointing Revival and Leadership Explosion Event in one conference that catapults the saints into higher dimensions of leadership, breakthrough, freedom, influence and impact.

www.12slm.org